KILTOLOGY

Words of Wisdom for the Kilted Universe

Volume 1

The Early Days

By Kevin M. Thompson

KiltsRock.com

Published by BOTK Publishing

Copyright © 2012 Kevin M. Thompson

ISBN: 098593820X

ISBN-13: 978-0-9859382-0-8

I am dedicating this book to a few folks who make my world go round. First my kids Quinn and Addison, both of whom provide me with more love than any one man should be allowed.

Second are my family and friends from around the world who have helped me through many tough times and continue to do so.

Third are my brothers of The Brotherhood of the Kilt, whose inspiration made this possible.

Last and possibly most important is a very close personal friend, Captain Owen Fogarty of the US Army. His loyalty and unending willingness to put the safety of his countrymen above his own makes me proud to know and support him. Keep your head down and powder dry, my friend.

-Kevin M. Thompson

CONTENTS

There are plenty of contents; I'm not listing them all here.

You will just have to read them yourself.

#1

Use sport shield often and always. Your balls will thank you.

#2

ALWAYS sweep your pleats when you sit down.

Cold, aluminum bleachers or plastic chairs against bare skin is bad at best; painful at worst if you get stuck. (A-la tongue to the frozen flagpole)

#3

Always be mindful of wind, especially when getting in and out of a car.

Even Mother Nature wants to get a glimpse of your kilted pride.

#4

Know that some folks want a picture of you in your kilt...with or without your knowledge or permission.

(This means the young co-ed who is not-so-discretely following you around is NOT trying to get a date or your number, just a pic to show her friends.)

#5

When standing up, always check your pleats.

Being the constant center of attention, having your pleats all out of sorts (especially if they are flipped up too high) is not the kind of attention you want, especially if pics wind up all over the internet.

#6

If you find the need to run while kilted, be sure you either slide your sporran to the side or hold it in one hand.

It is pointless to run if you arrive at your destination battered and broken.

#7

It is your kilt, wear it as you wish.

Anyone who tells you otherwise can fork over the hundreds or thousands of dollars necessary to meet their definition of "properly kilted". Living "properly kilted" is VERY expensive.

#8

Pleats in the back, period. No debate, questions or argument.

I don't care if you are the Bonnie Prince Charles himself, you will look like a complete buffoon if you wear the kilt with the apron in the back and pleats in the front.

This is your only warning. There ARE people in the world who will correct this glaring error, with or without your permission.

#9

When at a festival or event where kilties are present, do not start a fight.

It is most likely that the folks you are in conflict with are far better armed than whatever hired security force is present.

(And it would be real hard to explain to your friends that you got your ass kicked by a guy in a skirt.)

☙❧

#10

Please make sure you remove the basting stitches in your tartan kilt before venturing out in the world.

It's like wearing a suit to an interview and forgetting to take it out of the cleaner's bag.

(There is a tutorial on this here; I'll post the link when I find it.)

#11

Contrary to popular belief, there are situations where undergarments should (or must) be worn with a kilt.

Keep this in mind when kilting up, you don't want to spend any time in the lockup over a clothing decision.

#12

Good single malt whisky is to be enjoyed and savored, not pounded like plastic bottle liquors you find on the bottom shelf of some liquor stores.

If you are intent on doing shots of good aged single malt, keep these things in mind.

1. Your bar tab will be VERY high.
2. You will not be able to function for very long
3. Odds are, if you are kilted while doing this, there will be great stories in which you are the star and you will have no memory of them.
4. You will most likely feel like hell the next day or two unless you are a professional.

#13

When packing your sporran, be very mindful of the activities in which you plan to partake.

Wearing the equivalent of a daypack over your manhood during most any activity will ruin your day very quickly.

#14

If you want to kilt check someone, make sure you warn them and make sure they are ok with it.

You don't know how they will react. Some folks do not want a kilt check under any circumstance.

(This goes for men and women since kilts of one form or another are worn by both.)

#15

Be ever mindful of the overly-vocal self-proclaimed "Kilt expert".
They tend to be annoying know-it-alls.

You *are* wearing you kilt wrong, just ask them.

(If you want a real opinion about your kilt, go ask the guy in a kilt
who is NOT blathering about how much they know about kilts.
Odds are, they know more than most.)

#16

Contrary to popular belief, a kilt is a very poor substitute for a
parachute.

It would make for a better internet video, except for the landing.

#17

Kilt pins are pinned through the outer apron ONLY.

Pinning through both layers of the kilt will turn it into a potato sack, which is not much fun to walk in.

#18

Kilts are delivered with the following unwritten warnings, most of which are universally applicable and true:
~ Women will find you more attractive
~ You will have more self-confidence
~ You will be the center of attention (at least for a while)
~ Random people will talk to you all the time
~ Your photograph will be taken with and without your knowledge
~ You will be asked to conquer small countries
~ Everyone thinks you can play the pipes and throw the caber
~ You will have drinks bought for you at the pub
~ Your nether regions will become the topic of many discussions and thoughts everywhere you go
~ Your life will become far more eventful
~ You will eventually wind up at KiltsRock.com

#19

The kilt is the female equivalent of catnip.

Best part is, if it last more than four hours, simply call room service for more red bull.

#19

When using the bathroom, BE SURE you collect your pleats and keep them off the seat.

You really don't want any kling-ons on your kilt. They bring tribbles.

#20

It is of extreme importance that all kilties learn physical restraint and develop very thick "skin".

Being kilted in a bifurcated world makes you the target of an ignorant public's taunts and jeers.

(Those who don't have restraint and thick skin are usually pissed off all the time or in trouble for whacking someone over the head because his kilts was called a skirt.)

#21

When in the country kilted, be extra careful where you go.

Farmers may likely shoot you on sight to protect the sheep, still and their daughters.

#22

All your p@nt$ are suck.

#23

The Kilt is the perfect garment for long-distance driving.

No need to adjust every few miles.

#24

Kilts make great pillows,

especially if you are sharing.

#25

(For the non-kilted out there)

The bag a kiltie wears in front of his kilt is called a sporran.

It is not a man purse, murse, man bag or any other poorly-thought out derogatory term you come up with.

If you must make such a silly comment, be warned you will probably not like any response you get.

#26

Sucking on the corners of your kilt does NOT provide the same nutritional value as your towel.

You will most likely wind up with a hell of a hangover, though.

#27

Always carry two flasks when you plan to carry a flask.

One with your favorite single malt for you to enjoy as you wish.

The other with whatever you have laying around that you are not too fond of. This goes to mooches and "is that a flask you have there" types.

(Just make sure you can have a flask where ever you go. Don't want you getting in trouble over a wee nip.)

#28

Walking in to a strip club wearing a kilt may have the same effect on you as if you walked into a dog pound for aggressive dogs with a bloody T-bone steak around your junk.

Every dog wants your steak.

#29

The Kilties Creed (tip o' the hat to the USMC)
by KT

"This is my Kilt.

There are many like it, but this one is mine.

My Kilt is my best friend. It is my life. I must master it as I master my life.

My Kilt, without me, is useless. Without my Kilt, I am naked.

I must wear my Kilt true. "

#30

Donning the kilt is very zen in nature.

Chucking the kilt is not

#31

Any situation, especially one being photographed, can be made
infinity more interesting and/or humorous simply by adding a kilt!

#32

The simple presence of a man in a kilt has been known to quell uprisings and conflicts without a single fist being raised or shot being fired.

#33

Wool tartan kilts and washing machines mix about as well as 3 kilties and only one beer.

Translation: hand-wash your wool kilts!

#34

One of the only differences between a wool blanket and a traditional great kilt is what you find under it!

#35

While a kilt will instill great confidence, increase sell esteem and add insurmountable virility, it does not impart upon the wearer the powers of flight, laser-vision or make you bullet proof.

Yes, that means you only FEEL like a superhero. While you may draw in the ladies like the pied piper, you still can't fly.

#36

There is exactly one day of the year where the wearing of the kilt will without a doubt be misunderstood.

Halloween

If you wear it on Halloween, carry a recording device that can play "It's not a @#%@#$ costume!!!" You will go hoarse if you don't.

#37

No matter how powerful the kilt, it will not prevent some idiot on the other side of the world from picking up the phone and ruining your day.

(And no, you can't get your hand through the phone to fix their wagon. I tried; the holes in my phone are too small.)

#38

A kilt is only as spectacular as its wearer. Even the simplest of kilts can be made exquisite with the right attitude.

#39

Kilts are excellent at trapping hot air, especially in elevators.

Just don't move to fast until you exit. This way no one will pass out from the fumes until after you leave.

#40

Kittens, squirrels and moths are a kiltie's only natural enemies.

Everything else bows before the greatness that is the Kilt.

#41

When approaching a sleeping kiltie always take extreme care.

1. Make sure VERY strong coffee is brewing.
2. Have a flask at the ready.
3. If he is rather disheveled and still in his clothes from the night before, be sure the stick you poke him with is AT LEAST 10 feet long.
4. If at all possible, make sure you have a small team of special-ops kilties at the ready with some good boxty and a Guinness for breakfast.

#42

Be sure you are well armed when engaging in mental swordplay with
a Kiltie.

You never know what he is capable of, and it is most likely more
than you expect.

#43

Simply owning a kilt does not make you a kiltie. Just like a
thermometer and stethoscope doesn't make you a doctor.

You need to do a little research to know what you are wearing, and
how to wear it.

#44

Voluntary community service is something everyone should do, especially if they wear are kilted while doing it!

☙❧

#45

Here are a couple of thoughts on choosing footwear to wear with your kilt

1. Make sure they are COMFORTABLE!!!
2. If possible in the style you want, water resistant is good.
3. See #1
4. If you want few odd-comments from fashion "experts" try to match leathers if you can, but it is up to you completely.
5. If you haven't gotten the idea, see #1 again.
6. Make sure you are buying the footwear because you actually like them, and not because some kilt "expert" said "if you don't have this exact style shoe, you can't wear the kilt." The only reason you can't wear the kilt is if you don't actually have one.
7. See #1 one last time.

#46

When wearing a kilt in the rain, if the pleats get soaked be sure to wring them out.

Wet pleats beating on the back of your legs will wear your skin raw.

#47

The kilt is the great equalizer in the battle of the sexes, giving men the weapons needed to effectively combat "feminine wiles", rendering most women defenseless.

Basically it has the same effect as a shapely woman in a sundress standing between you and the sun.

Completely disarming.

#48

With all the power the kilt has, it has yet given me the clairvoyance enough to find the hidden kiltie base.

#49

It has been documented in many cases that a kilt may have the ability to create an Invisibility field around the wearer.

Some folk's brains can't handle the kilt, and just edit it out of reality.

#50

It has been proven without a doubt that kilties are ALL imbued with the ability to BS, prattle, yammer, and carry on about absolutely nothing for excessively long periods of time, with or without the presence of alcohol or anything actually interesting to talk about!

It is also widely known that the average kiltie's ability to tell grand stories of all manner is legendary, especially when in the presence of other kilties and bonnie lasses.

#51

When sitting in a kilt, be sure the apron falls properly between the legs. Wearing a Rob Roy style sporran will almost ensure this, although most any sporran will do.

The last thing any kiltie needs is someone complaining to the local constables about "some guy showing his bits and pieces in public."

#52

A kilt is only as funny as the fool wearing it.

Mind you, not every kiltie is a fool, so be careful who you make fun of. A sharp wit is far more painful than a blunt fist.

#53

For fear for life and limb, NEVER joke with a kiltie about a new kilt being on their doorstep.

You might wind up a fixture on said doorstep until the kilt arrives.

#54

No matter what you have been told, remember a kilt is only a piece of clothing.

It will not slay dragons, conquer armies or woo the lasses all by itself.

#55

There is nothing on this earth like a new kilt!!!

The kilt has strange and mysterious powers. Most are completely undocumented.

The best one is its ability to get people to buy you things or give you stuff for free without any words or suggestions by the wearer. I like that one a LOT.

(Yes, it is mostly at the pub...but it has happened in shops and at fairs a few times as well!)

#56

The Kilt is a great diet supplement.

If your kilt doesn't fit, hang it on the fridge door. If that leftover turkey or chocolate pudding pie is calling you, try the kilt on before you open the fridge.

If the kilt doesn't fit, don't open the door.

#57

Who is the luckier, the kiltie or the bonnie lass who checks him?

#58

A refrigerated sporran would be the apex of sporran design, if not for the constant clanging of the cooling system against the brass 'neath the kilt.

The wool kilt is one of the greenest, most environmentally and economically friendly pieces of clothing on the planet.

~ With care, it can last generations
~ With practice, it can be made by anyone who can use a needle
~ Wool kilts are made from renewable natural resources
~ The Kilt is a fashion statement of its own. it never goes out of style
~ It can be worn in all seasons
~ There is no need to buy a different kilt for every type of event or occasion
~ There are no landfills overflowing with discarded kilts (if you know of one, let me know!)

#60

The wearing of the Kilt can have therapeutic properties, both physical and psychological.

~ Wearing a kilt generally increased the level of activity, as sitting in a kilt isn't much fun
~ Increased attention by the opposite sex can increase one's self esteem
~ Increased self-confidence is a common result of wearing a kilt
~ Kilt wearing reduces heat and pressure in the nether regions, which can possibly increase fertility and/or virility
~ Kilts, as a rule, are simply awesome

#61

The Kilt is perfect holiday camouflage.

You can spill almost any amount of punch or fruitcake on it, and most folks probably wouldn't notice!

In some cases, you can even stand next to the Christmas tree and vanish altogether!

#62

No matter what you do, always remember where your glow in the dark kilt is.

If you don't, it wills scare the hell out of you when you walk into the room and see a glowing kilt just floating there.

#63

Make sure your sporran is properly adjusted when you put it on. Too high and it will ram into your belt constantly which is annoying. Too low and you will whack yourself in the junk or the sporran will bounce around between your legs which is even more annoying.

#64

The wearing of the kilt will not make you stronger, better or faster...

...but it will sure as hell LOOK like you are!

#65

A few days ago a guy walked up to me and said "Holy Crap! You're wearing a kilt!"

I said "Holy Crap! Your ass is on fire!" and walked away.

#66

When making a kilt purchase for wear in wet or cold climates, 100% wool is your best bet.

It will keep you warm and dry, even if the kilt itself gets wet. Most other fabrics will either leave you cold and wet or sweltering because there is no air flow.

#67

Walking over or near and open fire while kilted is a very bad idea
unless you're really know what you are doing.

A few wisps of fire up the kilt will certainly ruin your day,
ESPECIALLY if you've been eating Mexican food!

#68

For want of shelter, a wandering kiltie offered his kilt to keep a few
of the local lasses out of the rain.

From that moment on, kilts became FAR more prevalent amongst
men seeking the company of the ladies, as those without one slept
cold and alone in the rain.

#69

He said "69"

#70

The Kilt is the only known garment that is an effective defense against the blamethrower.

Anyone with the cojones to blame the guy in a kilt for anything beside the ladies and beer disappearing needs their head examined.

#71

Whilst shoveling snow in a kilt, be ever mindful of snowplows.

Icy mush coming off that plow blade is hell on the legs...worse if it happens to get up under the kilt.

#72

I have found proof that a masculine male in a kilt is NOT the only form of dress that will get extremely strange looks and comments which are not overtly sought.

Walk around a town in the south the day after a blizzard in a pair of shorts and sweatshirt. You can actually see some folk's brains lock-up trying to understand what they are seeing.

(I didn't want to get any road-salt on the kilt this time 'round.)

#73

Kiltology, the study of kilts and kilting, is best done in the company of several bonnie lasses.

Studying anything is more fun with bonnie lasses.

#74

Wearing a kilt on New Year's Day will bring you luck.

(Most likely it will bring luck of some sort on every other day as well!)

#75

The threads of a tartan are far more than simply colored wool woven together. The tartan as a whole represents a family. The threads are its members...brothers, sisters, mothers, fathers and so on. The tighter the weave, the stronger the fabric and the longer the tartan will last.

The same goes for a family.

The tighter a family stays together, the longer it will last. There will be no holes in the tartan or broken threads that cannot be mended with a gentle and steady hand.

A tartan is a family united as one, with each thread adding to the fabric, helping it grow and remain strong.

#76

Not even the greatest kilt will keep you warm forever if all you do is sit on your ass all day long instead of going somewhere and doing something.

#77

A kilt does not have any mystical powers to help fix your melon or deal with most medical issues.

BUT

Get enough kilties in the same place at the same time, and you will almost always forget you had any problems to start with!

(Especially a few I'd rather not name here. They can talk enough BS to make your head spin right off!)

#78

A kilt will make a great pillow in a pinch.

Just be sure you are careful where you sleep. Unexpected pillow fluffing can have wildly varied results.

#79

The kilt has many curative properties. It can effectively treat fat, ugly and odd.

With all its greatness, unfortunately, it cannot treat stupid. Stupid is as stupid does, not much can be done about that.

#80

When it hits the fan, make sure you only lift the over-apron to shield your face.

Getting anything under the kilt at velocity is not recommended in any situation.

#81

If properly positioned and manipulated, a kilt can serve as a good substitute for a broken or missing female support apparatus. (Commonly known as the "over the shoulder boulder holder.")

The tricky part is how to get around without taking the kilt off or breaking local decency laws.

#82

How to make a kilt lamp

1. Buy string of battery-powered LED lights. DO NOT buy incandescent lights as you will get burned BADLY.
2. Affix LED light strings to underside of kilt about 1/2 of the way up the kilt. Safety pins will work if nothing else is available.
3. Affix switch within reach without having to reach up the kilt.
4. Put on kilt and walk into dimly lit location with lots of lasses.
5. Turn on light switch and watch the riotous fun begin.

#83

I once heard someone say they had enough kilts, and didn't need any more.

As all kilties know, this is an impossible statement. The minute you think you have enough kilts you will discover a new kilt you have to have.

ᘓᘒ

#84

When making kilted interstellar flights, be sure you wear a modern kilt with pockets or have belt pouches and stow the sporran in your luggage.

Sporrans and zero gravity are NOT a good combination.

#85

Avoid water slides while kilted, especially if regimental.

High-pressure enemas are not fun.

#86

Hiding in your kilt will not stop the world from turning.

It will, however, get you a LOT of silly looks.

#87

Your footwear is one of the most important parts of your kilt accessories kit.

If you have crappy footwear, you will be miserable if you plan on standing for more than a few minutes.

When selecting your footwear, be 100% certain they are comfortable. There is no amount of single malt that can fix shoes that don't fit well.

#88

Burns Night is evil.

Plain and simple.

#89

Kilts and computers work exceptionally well together, especially when you kilt up and leave the computer at home as you venture out into the world to experience all it has to offer.

#90

While a kilt is hardy, strong and very tough

WASH THE DAMN FOOL THING ONCE A WHILE!!!

A kilt that can stand by itself will most likely try to get into your fridge, eat your food, drink you drink and shag the lady of the house without you!

#91

Coffee is a kilties second best friend.

I don't know who or what your best friend is, but a cup of good coffee will almost always make a morning more bearable.

#92

Life is really short.

Hike up your kilt, lose the p@nt$, quit being a pansy-ass and do something with yourself.

Otherwise I'll just find you when I need a place to park my bike.

#93

When storing your kilt, be 100% certain you do not put your kilt in with your lassie's mini-kilts.

Last time I saw this happen, the kilt got the $#%^$% kicked out of it for trying to get a peek up the mini-kilt.

#94

Regardless of your pedigree, you will always find one pain in the ass that "is more Scottish than you are."

If you encounter this person, just let it go. Fighting a match of wits is no fun when your competition comes to the fight unarmed.

#95

Be wary of snow drifts.

The kilt may be more or less snow proof on the outside, but get some snow on the inside of the kilt, you might just freeze the wedding tackle!

#96

When making snow angels while kilted, be sure to sweep your pleats as you lay down and be very mindful of the wind.

The probability of both your kilt flying up and freezing your bits and pieces are very high if you don't.

#97

What is the difference between p@nt$ and a kilt?

A pair of p@nt$ which is filthy, battered, worn and beat to hell is generally retired to the oil-change rag bin as they are near the end of their useful life.

A kilt in the same condition is most likely just recovering from a festival or kilt night and is simply in need of a washing before the next kilt night.

#98

If ever you see a poor soul wearing his kilt with the pleats in front, I beg of you to gently inform him that the pleats go in back so he can save what pride he has left.

Kilties don't let kilties kilt backwards.

(Yes, I need to make a bumper sticker with that on it, and fast!)

#99

It is well know that the kilt has mysterious powers over the lasses and may enable the wearer to accomplish otherwise impossible tasks.

The kilt does not, however, have any powers over illness brought home for your kid's daycare. You will have to fight that battle on your own.

(As suggested by one daycare provider, "water of life" may have curative properties according to her Scottish relatives.)

#100

Kilties of old were very forward thinking.

Only a bunch of guys in kilts could come up with the perfect computer repair tool: a caber.

#101

Deconstructing a kilt is at the same time one of the most painful and fulfilling things you can do.

It is extremely time consuming, and requires patience and a steady hand to reduce a kilt to its basic parts: tartan, buckles, leather and a pile of broken string. It hurts to do this, but at the same time it is a wonderful thing to know this tartan is freed from its torture and will be used to create a wonderful new kilt which can be properly enjoyed for a great many years to come.

#102

A new kilt is little protection from the fear of losing a loved one, no matter how well made it is.

#103

Whilst kilted, peeing in the wind is the least of your problems.

Managing your sporran and kilt while trying not to expose your kilted pride to the world or hose yourself down is the real trick.

#104

The caffeine content of the average kilt is not enough to keep you awake if you are tired.

I suggest finding other means of awakening, just be careful if you ask the lasses for something to get you going.

#104

One kilt Two Kilt Three Kilt Four.

Why, bonnie lass, is my kilt on the floor?

#105

(Stands aloft in front of the kilted masses)

"As I walk through the Valley of the Shadow of Death, I shall fear no evil.

For I am the baddest kiltie in the whole %@#$%@ valley!"

(And there was much rejoicing)

#106

Hazelnut spread and bagels go great with kilts....as long as you don't get any ON the kilt.

Hazelnut spread is a major pain to get out of a wool kilt.

#107

Be wary of any kilted Easter bunnies you may happen upon.

Scotch Eggs are supposed to come from chickens, not rabbits!!!

#108

Kilts and leather go together like peanut butter and jelly.

(Especially if you have the kilt and your bonnie lass has the leather!!)

#109

A kilt is a piece of fabric. It does not make the man.

The decisions he makes, the actions he takes and words he speaks
make the man.

However, the Kilt *does* make him look bad-ass when he does it!

#110

If you view the world through the eyes of a child, the kilt is a really cool piece of clothing with endless possibilities.

If you view the world through the eyes of a man jaded by society, "proper education", a bad job and peer pressure, you will most likely see the kilt as a deviant costume worn by miscreants.

I'm still trying to figure out what I want to be when I grow up, so the possibilities are still endless!

#111

Here is one for the lasses.

One of the most effective means of attracting a kilted man from across the room without breaking any decency laws is to wear tartan. More or less is completely up to you, and can have varying effects depending on how you wear it.

The tartan itself shows you love the kilt more than because "there are no drawers under there."

#112

Even the stoutest kilt provides no protection from the calling of a
box of frozen tag-alongs.

#113

Tartan is the physical representation of a family.

The actions and words of the people in that family are what define
the family, NOT the tartan or its description and meaning.

#114

Whilst using the toilet kilted, be sure you gather your kilt up around you or hang it on the door while taking care of business.

There is nothing worse than a filthy kilt...especially if it isn't your filth.

಼಼಼಼

#115

The very best way to bring your newborn baby home is wrapped in a length of tartan.

My son was welcomed into the world wrapped in MacTavish.

It is widely accepted knowledge that the Kilt is the second most useful item in the universe.

~ It keeps you dry when it rains
~ It keeps you warm when it is cold
~ It keeps you shaded when it is sunny
~ It keeps you protected when assaulted by weather or nature
~ It keeps you entertained by drawing in curious people
~ It keeps you...umm......"active" with the ladies (see above)
~ It keeps you safe (First rule of warfare - "Don't screw with the guy in the kilt")
~ It keeps you fed (I always seem to get free stuff whilst kilted)
~ It keeps your wallet from going empty (see above)

Of course, it is #2 because the most useful item in the universe is the Towel. The single factor that prevents the kilt from being #1 is this: There is no way in hell I'm going to dip my kilt in nutrients so I can suck on the edges when I get hungry. Not going to happen.

#117

You mind is your own worst enemy.

To defeat this most dastardly of foes, don your kilt, find some kilties and cause a scene just by showing up at your favorite social place.

The mind simply can't handle such nonsensical loneliness!

#118

A kilt's worst enemy is NOT the moth, scissors or even the occasional intoxicated pub patron who can't hold their liquor.

A kilt's worst enemy is the small child.

The pleats on a kilt seem to look very much like a swing set or monkey bars. Many a kilt have been badly damaged at the hands of one particular little monkey who thinks it is funny to swing from pleat to pleat while dodging daddy's efforts to remove said monkey from his kilt.

#119

When driving long distance (meaning more than about half an hour) ALWAYS wear a kilt. Modern kilt designs work best as pleats are usually sewn-down, and there is far less bulk in the pleats.

1. No adjusting
2. See #1
3. Floor AC vents keep you VERY cool in the summer heat
4. See #1
5. Makes for very interesting pit stops in more remote locations
6. See #1
7. Road-side pit stops are far easier
8. Did I mention see #1?
9. No problems with funky smells after sitting for many hours on end
10. If you didn't get the hint yet... NO ADJUSTING!!!

#120

The kilt is easily the perfect garment for long trips, by auto or by foot. In the car there is no adjusting, and on the trail, there is no massive concoction of fabric chaffing your skin and soaking up mud and water.

p@nt$ are evil.

#121

The wearing of the kilt is a well-known natural remedy for introversion. It will either cure the pour soul who despises being the limelight or force them to give up the kilt altogether.

As far as I know, introversions cured by kilt rates are stable at 100%.

#122

Be very careful when tightening your kilt straps. Make no illusion as to how big you are. Tightening the straps as a means to decrease your width will drastically shorten the life of your kilt, and possibly make you look rather silly if any stitching were to burst suddenly while out and about.

#123

The freedom given by the Kilt comes at a cost.

Whilst answering Nature's Call out in the wilderness, be ever mindful of where you are and what is around you. Insects, small animals and toxic plants tend to gravitate to the underside of the kilt like a dog to steak. BE CAREFUL!!!

(Mosquitoes, gnats and poison ivy are the most common offenders in wooded regions of the world.)

#124

"Only after the last tree has been cut down... Only after the last river has been poisoned... Only after the last fish has been caught, only then will you find that money cannot be eaten."

- Cree Indian Prophecy

(how does this apply to kilts? Not sure but it makes one hell of a point.)

#125

The power of the kilt is endless, but it is the man in the kilt who turns that power into something useful.

#126

"Never go up a ladder in a kilt" is something I've heard myself and on the web a great many times.

I've noticed one very obvious issue with this statement: I've only ever heard or seen it come from men in p@nt$!

#127

The kilt is more than just a garment. The wearing of the tartan is the same as waving your own family flag. In a historical context, the wearing of the kilt displays where you are from and to whom your allegiances lie with.

The only known difference is a flag has a huge pole under it, and even that is a hotly debated topic.

#128

Be extremely mindful of a kilt left wet too long.

You will know yours needs to be dried when the back of your knees
feel like they are being sanded by your pleats. This is an
EXTREMELY unpleasant experience.

#129

The kilt makes a very poor alarm clock. If anything, it helps promote
sleeping longer!

#130

Kilts and fast food seldom mix.

Not only is the possibility of getting condiments or other bit of food on the kilt extremely high, if you eat too much fast food your kilt will find a home in the back of your closet, unworn!

#131

In its simplicity and functionality, the kilt is nearly the perfect garment. It is not only extremely usable and durable; it is in many ways artful and creative.

That being said, it is common for people to affix just about anything to a kilt just because they can.

#132

When selecting a kilt belt, be brutally honest with yourself about your waist size. Make sure it has a little wiggle room, both up and down in size.

A kilt belt alone has absolutely no slimming effects, none at all.

Besides, you really don't want to look like a bolt of fabric squeezed too tight in the middle!

#133

The wearing of the kilt does not, in itself, entitle it's wearer to anything.

If you want to be entitled to something, get off your butt and make it happen.

There is no such thing as a free kilt.

#134

There was once a rumor of a band of kilted ninjas.

It is still a rumor, as no one has ever seen a kilted ninja and lived to talk about it.

#135

The kilt has been and can still be considered a weapon of war. On the battle field it is a weapon of demoralization. Any army seeing a group of kilt-clad warriors yelling and charging in a seemingly insane manner would flee.

In modern times it is a weapon in the war for the fairer sex. Unleashing a kilt in a public setting (especially where a large number of people are congregated) will have the same effect as dropping a bomb on all the males in the vicinity. Their chance of getting any attention from the lasses drops exponentially when in the presence of a kilted gent. If there are two kilties or more, the non-kilted may as well go home, as there would be little chance they would have any success.

#136

If ever you are in need, in a bad spot or otherwise not doing well, do not forget your kilted brethren. They are your family.

(Even if you try to forget about them, there isn't a snowball's chance in hell they will let you!)

#137

The internet is probably the single worst method of communication ever created.

Yes, if makes it possible to communicate with people instantly all over the world.

BUT

With a majority of communication between people being non-verbal, the internet makes it EXTREMELY easy for your words to be misunderstood.

The wisdom part - be careful in choosing your words. Not to avoid offense or limit your expression, but to be sure the intent of your messages is painfully obvious. Put simply, if you are talking about a duck, call it a ^#$%^# duck.

The other wisdom part - don't take anything personally. Misunderstanding on the web is about as common as keys on a keyboard. Everything you read must be fully understood before you decide to tear someone a new one. It could have simply been a poorly worded joke instead of an outright attack.

(Also, the use of smileys helps with the intent, especially if your messages are in jest or not meant to be taken literally.)

#138

Never let yourself go unkilted for too long.

All the additional attention could be a serious shock to your system,
which is NOT a good thing

#139

You ARE your brother's keeper.

What does that mean?

Exactly what it says.

It is your responsibility to look out for your friends and family, no
matter how much they may piss you off or go insane. If you do not
help your friends when they need it most (whether they ask for help
or not), who is going to be there when you need help? If tough love
is the only help that will work, then so be it. True friends and family
do not abandon one another.

Another of the extremely short list of things best NOT done in a kilt is changing a very active baby's diaper.

The odds of getting something on your kilt are extremely high, especially if it is a boy or the baby isn't feeling good.

Getting that out of a kilt is no fun either, worse than enduring the changing itself!

(Old school wood clothespins DO work on the nose....I've used several)

CB EO

#141

The definition of a "clean kilt" varies from person to person.

A kilt has the ability to appear clean to all but the most discerning individual when it has not been cleaned in a very long time, if ever.

Word of advice: even if it looks and smells clean, wash you kilt every once a while. You can be surprised how much filth is hidden in those threads.

(I washed a wool kilt I thought was clean once. It went through four rounds of hand washing before the water wasn't black from the filth hidden in the kilt. I now wash any kilts I wear often enough to know they aren't gaining consciousness.)

#142

Contrary to popular belief, if you stare a kilt long enough you will NOT see a sailboat or some other image hidden in the tartan.

(There have been occasions where lasses staring at a kilt have seen something they didn't expect, but that is a different discussion altogether.)

#143

Unless you are playing with Kiltie Rules, do not play baseball kilted. Sliding into anything on gravel in a kilt is just asking for trouble and a trip to the hospital to pull the gravel out of your arse!

(By Kiltie rules, sliding is not allowed, but the fielders can tackle the runners if needed.)

#144

When you are squatting or kneeling kilted, be ever mindful of what is under you.

Traditional wool kids are like magnets to all sorts of muck, dirt and vegetation.

Sitting with a thistle stuck to the inside of the kilt is not something I have any desire repeat.

#145

When picking you battles, keep in mind that no matter what there will be a fight of some kind.

Any battle that doesn't involve a fight is not a battle. It is surrender.

#146

When a wee laddie says "Daddy, I want a kilt" GET OFF YER ARSE AND GET ONE FOR THE WEE BOY!!!

The sooner he learns the greater glories of being a kiltman, the better!! (Although you might want to keep the lasses away for a bit whilst he learns about pleat sweeping, Mother Nature and proper sitting technique)

#147

Be ever vigilant in the maintenance of your kilt and kit. Even the most expensive and well-made product will be useless in a short amount of time if you do not take care of your gear.

In a nutshell, WASH THAT FOUL, FILTHY KILT!

#148

Your friends and family are the only folks who will help you when
you fall.

Don't piss on them and run them off. Falling on your ass alone
sucks.

#149

Trust and respect, once lost, are very hard to regain.

Word to the wise: don't screw it up like I did.

#150

Sleep, when lost, can never be found again. It's just gone.

If someone wakes you up for no good reason, be very clear in your intentions to place their cranium adjacent to their coccyx if they do it again.

(Oh, a folded wool kilt makes an excellent pillow, so long as the buckles are not poking you in the face!)

#151

Be ever vigilant in your studies of history and the mistakes of those who have already made them.

You don't want to be the fool who repeats an epic failure.

#152

When putting your kilt pin on, for the love of Pete make sure you only pin through the outer apron. If you pin through both the inner and outer apron, you turn your kilt into some kind of strange wool body-sack.

(If you don't, you will eventually rip the hell out of the kilt!)

#153

Seek not to bathe in riches of gold and silver, but to live in the riches of the hearts and souls those around you.

The riches of family and love

#154

Ferris wheels are the enemy of a great many kiltie.

It usually causes great public disruption, as crowds may gather beneath to get a glimpse of your kilted pride as your car goes around.

(Then again, if you are a single kiltie, it may be your best friend as the lasses wait for you to disembark.)

#155

42

#156

one kilt,
two kilt,
three kilt,
four

five kilt,
six kilt,
seven kilt
more

one kilt,
two kilt,
three kilt...

claymore?

#157

If you have something to say to someone, say it.

Should you decide to avoid the situation and keep quiet, it is your own damn fault if things don't go the way you want and you get pissed off.

(Luckily this rarely applies to kilties. I don't know a single one who holds their tongue!)

#158

Instead of spending all your time trying to place blame for a problem, focus on fixing the problem.

It doesn't matter who did what until AFTER the problem is fixed, and then only to prevent the problem from happening again. Every second spent trying to find fault is a second the problem still exists.

(One of these days our society will figure this out as a whole and everyone's life will be MUCH better, but I don't expect it any time soon.)

(The kids made me think of this. One spilled a drink and was trying to blame the other instead of cleaning up the mess. It will take a few more tries, but they will learn.)

#159

Be mindful of what you put in your sporran, especially rob roy style sporrans. If it is too heavy or has pointy objects in it, you can potentially cause pain or injury to yourself and/or your kilt.

It is especially important if you may have to move quickly. A heavy swinging sporran can be very dangerous to the wearer.

#160

Find joy in everything you do, no matter how mundane, difficult or a pain in the arse it might be.

A life without joy is no fun at all.

(Just be careful, Joy tends to get a little randy when in the company of kilties. Also watch your flask, she loves islay single malt!)

#161

Boredom is the silent crusher of souls.

Be sure you do something exciting and fulfilling every day, no matter how big or small. Extra points if you do it in a kilt AND make a lass blush.

#162

When trying to stay warm kilted, make sure you have a heavy kilt, thick jacket, good hat and WARM socks. You don't need leggings unless you are planning a trip with the Inuit.

(Single malt and a bonnie lass also go a long way to staying warm, but are not as easy to obtain and keep around!)

#163

Mediocrity is the path to certain boredom and blah-ness.

Strive every day to lead an exceptional life, making a positive impact on others and kilting to the best of your ability!

#164

For better or worse always hold true to your own beliefs and ideals.

If you don't, you become little more than a yes-man, trying to please everyone and not living your life for yourself.

Strap on the kilt and be your own person. You have to live with the results of your actions, best hope they are your own.

#165

It is way too damn early for me to be up.

#166

Do not wait for the "perfect time" or "perfect situation" to do something you really want to do. If you wait for the perfect time, it will never come.

Get out there and do it. The perfect time is now.

#167

There is a reason many people think we kilt-wearers are more than a little crazy.

Who else would come up with the idea to throw trees to see who could flip it over straight? What about the insanity we call Golf?

Don't forget the wonderfulness called Single Malt Whisky...some of which tastes like drinking a burning log (my favorite ones, naturally).

It takes a certain type of person to find these things enjoyable, and I'm glad to count myself as one of them!

#168

Work to live, do not live to work.

We are not on this earth to provide cheap labor for someone else. If you have a thankless job, do everything you can to ensure you live a fruitful and enjoyable life away from work.

Do not allow yourself to be chained to that which pays the mortgage.

(Wearing a kilt while working may help you enjoy your job a LOT)

#169

Before you try to fix the universe, make sure you fix yourself first.

No way can you do any good if you are broken to start with.

#170

The ability of wool kilt pleats to pick up dirt, sticks and junk makes Velcro look like oiled stainless steel.

Make sure you check your pleats after squatting for whatever reason. Sitting on a stick or thistle isn't something I recommend.

#171

Kilts and motorcycles have a lot on common. Both are usually extremely cool, both can exude masculinity, and both should be used with extreme care.

Both should NOT be used at the same time unless you are EXTREMELY careful, and do not have a belt or chain driven bike.

Last think you want is for your kilt to be ripped off your body at 45mph or more. The conversation with the Police officer would be REALLY interesting, and the video would go viral in minutes!

#172

While every day is a good day to wear the kilt, any day in autumn is the best.

~ You can wear the 16-21oz wools without overheating
~ It isn't so cold that you need a foot-thick jacket
~ Many Oktoberfest brews are available
~ Many bonnie lasses develop the need to snuggle or otherwise warm themselves with a man in a kilt! (Best hope their hands aren't TOO cold!)

CB ఴ

#173

On the wearing of glow-in-the-dark kilts

~ There is no such thing as "it's dark under there"
~ EVERYONE will know you are there
~ They get hot really fast
~ If you are regimental, it is assured that anyone who thinks they may have seen your kilted pride actually did
~ Make sure you don't give away any free beer. You will not be able to avoid anyone coming back for more
~ You WILL get offers for a kilt check
~ Hiding from someone is simply not an option
~ Wild haggis will hunt you down. A Glow-in-the-dark kilt for a Wild Haggis is like catnip for cats. You won't win this one.

#174

Your kilted brethren are incredibly intelligent and wise. Be sure to always ask them if you have a problem or need help. It will save you a LOT of time wasted fumbling around trying to work a problem someone else has already solved.

They can also help with the tab after you celebrate your success at the local kilt-friendly pub!

#175

Buttery Popcorn and the Kilt are bitterest of enemies.

While the kilt is resilient to most every attack out there, the oily, salty residue from a massive tub of theatre popcorn can wreak havoc on your kilt.

#176

The kilt is one of the best known defenses in a snowball fight. Not only are you impervious to most anything that can be hurled your way, you can taunt you enemy at a moment notice which can cause serious psychological trauma to the enemy!

#177

Rid yourself of your sporran chains as soon as possible!

Get a set of leather sporran straps so those nasty chains will no longer tear, wear and otherwise destroy your precious kilt!

To add humor and a huge self-confidence boost, try the following

1. Strap on the kilt and go to a common public place known to have a lot of women (malls are good for this)
2. Walk around normally. (as if shopping, if in the mall)
3. When you pass a woman or group of women who apparently get quiet when they notice you in a kilt, let them pass.
4. Give them a two second count and turn around. Odds are you will catch them looking back at you.

This is a great morale booster and can be really funny if they forget where they are walking and hit a wall or some other inanimate object.

#179

If your kilt-belt size is around 34-36 inches, which happens to be the midpoint between kilt belt sizes that I have seen, get the larger belt and cinch it down to the smallest size, trimming the excess strapping inside the belt.

If you get the smaller belt, you will almost certainly need to buy another one at some point in the future.

(This only applies to traditional kilt belts. Some companies have similar belts with Velcro attachments instead of straps and buckles. These Velcro belts are far less troublesome in this regard.)

#180

There is no force in the known universe more destructive than a 4 year boy on a sugar high and his baby sister. Here are some tips to survive their onslaught

~ Do not let them swing on your pleats or kilt belt.
~ Keep them out of your sporran at all costs.
~ Kilts pins are deadly weapons in their hands. Keep them away.
~ Sgains are just plain out of the question.
~ Tails on a Prince Charlie jacket are one step removed from the olympic rings. Nothing good comes from their presence.
~ Flasks become expensive projectiles. Keep them out of sight.
~ Ghillie shoe laces are jump ropes and trip lines. Best kept tied tight.

൧൫

#181

When tending to young children, especially those who are just learning to walk, ALWAYS wear your sporran.

Suffice it to say that all children learning to walk are amateur Fred Astaires. And they LOVE tap dancing where they shouldn't!!!

(No...It isn't any fun at all, and I wasn't wearing the sporran this morning when Addy was 'dancing'.)

#182

When you get a new leathers sporran, be sure you talk to the sporran maker about a leather sealant to apply to the back of the sporran.

If you don't apply some kind of leather sealant, the leather dye will slowly rub into your kilt. It will discolor lighter color kilts if you are not careful.

(Last thing you want is a huge dark stain on your crotch!)

#183

Be extremely careful when wearing a large belt buckle with your kilt, especially if it had some form of raised embellishment (like a thistle).

It is very easy for you to accidentally put a scratch or gouge in any wood, leather or soft metal items, such as the rail of a cherry baby crib.

Odds are the buckle will fair far better than most wooden furniture!

#184

How a kiltie cures a headache

Option 1: Single malt Whisky

OR (for the non-drinker or when the bottle is empty)

Option 2: Imagine the agony of the p@nt$. It dulls any other pain.

#185

How to treat chaffing:

1. Single Malt and sport shield

or (for the non-drinker or owner of an empty bottle)

2. Sport Shield, less walking, going home, putting on p@nt$, dealing with it the hard way or sitting on ice.

#186

Do not attempt to placate two or more children under the age of 5 without candy, television, new toys every few minutes or some kind of clown with a dancing animal.

You will wind up insane, exhausted and you kilt will be reduced to short individual threads of destroyed wool.

(It would be easier to try to get the barkeep to give you free single malt all night!)

#187

Never EVER under any circumstances wake a sleeping kiltie unless you are 100% ready to deal with the consequences.

It can be far more dangerous than waking any animal from their slumber, especially if it is before noon on a weekend!

(I can't be certain, but I wouldn't be surprised if at least one of the major Scottish military victories over the ages was won simply because the enemy tried to engage them too early in the morning, and one soldier was upset that he was roused from his slumber!)

#188

It is a little known fact that one of the safest places on earth is with a man in a kilt.

There are very few people who are willing to admit "they got their ass kicked by a man in a skirt".

#189

All kilties beware of women bearing leaf blowers.

Nothing good will come of an encounter with a blushing lass with a wind machine.

(Well, almost nothing!)

#190

Next time you are at a Scottish/Celtic/medieval festival, seek out the blacksmith. He can make you a very cool iron bottle opener that you can attach to the draw string of your rob roy style sporran.

A kiltie without a bottle opening is one who will most likely break the bottle.

#191

Some tried and true means of getting the attention of a kiltie without calling it a skirt:

1. Kilt check (warm hands are best)
2. Single Malt (does not work all the time. There are many non-drinking kilties)
3. Boobies (also works for pretty much any other person who enjoys the female form, regardless of clothing)
4. Free food (works almost as well as #3)
5. Say "Sweet kilt. Is that a (insert tartan name for trads, kiltmaker for modern kilts)?"

#192

Applying the traditional kiltie repair methods to modern technology is not recommended unless said device is complete useless or really pissed you off.

Besides, bashing your expensive tech toys with a large object only gets more expensive as you attempt to "repair" them further.

#193

The kilt has a very unique sound-deadening power.

If you wear the kilt in a public area, you can usually observe a 10 foot circle around you where it is very quiet regardless of how many people there are.

It also seems to cause a dramatic increase in talk about 30 or so feet behind you.

I'm not aware of any other clothing that can do this outside the nudie bar.

#194

There are a few things the average kiltie can do to completely enrage their wives.

1. Leave the kilt hose hanging on the shower rod to dry
2. Eat too much haggis before going to bed (makes bad mexican food look like child's play)
3. Let the kids run rampant all day while she is at work, feeding them sugary foods and soda, and then tell her you are going out with the guys when she gets home.

To preserve your life and well-being, I suggest #3 be avoided at all costs. You could wind up an ex-kiltie, or worse, p@nted!

#195

We all know kids can break anything...but this is a first.

Keep your sporran drawstrings under close watch around children who like to swing on things, the strings can (and do) break under stress.

(Speaking of which, I'll be talking to Donnie about how to fix my BotK Wyvern drawstrings.)

#196

How far does a kiltie go into the woods?

As far as the first tree.

Any farther and there is no way passing lasses will see him to give him a blue ribbon!

#197

Every kiltie knows that if you are going to do anything that requires a trip to the hardware store, plan to two trips.

It has been proven time and time again that Mr. Murphy sits at the entrance to every hardware store in the land, imposing his law on all of us.

(There is also that cute lassie on checkout #4 who loves the kilt!)

#198

Wear your Kilt with pride today. Many kilties fought and died in wars which allow us the freedom to wear the kilt.

Respect those serving now and those who have fallen to protect us.

#199

When grocery shopping with your wife while wearing a kilt, do not let her leave her purse in the cart you are pushing around the store while she runs after something that was forgotten.

It causes many concerned stares from fellow shoppers, especially if it is one of those massive "everything but the kitchen sink will fit in here" type of things.

#200

Irish coffee and donuts (with real coffee) is the order of the day.

Don't ever get between a kiltie and his first coffee of the day.

It is one of the primary reasons the Darwin Awards have so many applicants!

KiltsRock.com

ABOUT THE AUTHOR

Kevin Thompson is an Eagle Scout, member of the Pi Kappa Alpha Fraternity, has various degrees and a passion for wearing kilts. Kevin founded the Brotherhood of the Kilt in 2007 to provide a supportive gathering place for other "kilties". After many adventures in kilting, including helping to raise the World's Largest Kilt on the Tulsa Driller, he has donated his summer vacation to the Survival Program at Old Rochester Regional Junior High School since 1988, but he says that nothing brings him joy like his two children.

Kevin has recorded his pearls of wisdom about kilting on his website for years, and here for the first time he has compiled the various articles in one place. Kevin, and his brothers and sisters of the kilt, hope you enjoy this book.

Made in the USA
Lexington, KY
11 October 2015